Aa

apple

Trace and print **A** and **a**.

The anteater admires ants gathering acorns.
Circle the ants. Count the acorns.

Bb

banana

Trace and print **B** and **b**.

B B

b b

A brown bear takes a bubble bath.

Color all the **B** spaces **blue**. Color all the **b** spaces **black**.

Cc

carrot

Trace and print **C** and **c**.

C C

c c

A calico cat naps on a cozy couch.
Connect the dots and color.

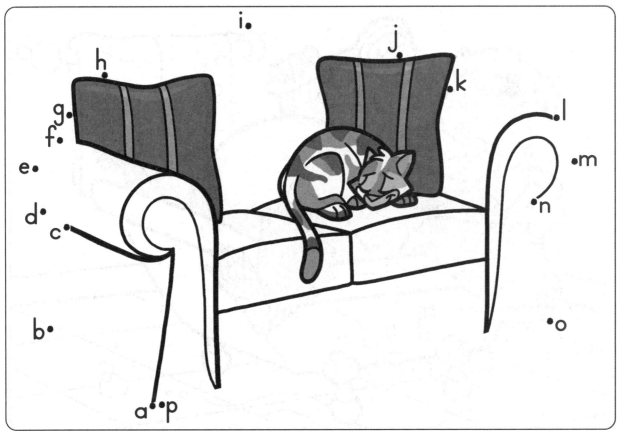

Dd

dill pickle

Trace and print **D** and **d**.

D D

d d

Dinosaurs play and dine in the dark den.
Circle the dinosaur that is different.

Ee

egg

Trace and print **E** and **e**.

E E

e e

An eager elephant drinks at the water's edge.
Connect the dots and color.

F f

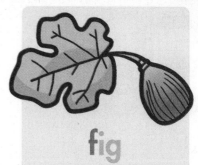

fig

Trace and print **F** and **f**.

F   F

f   f

A funny fish finds a friend.
Help the fish through the maze.

Start

Finish

Gg

grapes

Trace and print **G** and **g**.

G   G

g   g

Gray goats graze on green grass.
Color the goats **gray**.

Hh

honey

Trace and print **H** and **h**.

The happy horse wears a hat.
Connect the dots and color.

8

Draw lines to match the letter pairs.

A   B   C   D

d   c   b

E   F   G   H

h   g   e   f

I i

ice cream

Trace and print **I** and **i**.

Iggy the iguana visits India.
Find and circle 5 hidden iguanas.

J j

jelly

Trace and print **J** and **j**.

Sleepy jaguars rest in the jungle.
Add black spots to the jaguars.

K k

kiwifruit

Trace and print **K** and **k**.

K K

k k

Katie the kangaroo likes to fly kites.
Draw a kite.

L l

lemon

Trace and print **L** and **I**.

Liam the lion looks for Lucy the lioness.
Help the lion through the maze.

Start

Finish

Mm

mango

Trace and print **M** and **m**.

M M M

m m m

Monty the moose munches in the meadow.

Draw antlers for the moose.

Nn

noodles

Trace and print **N** and **n**.

N N

n n

Nancy the nightingale nears her nest.
Color and count the eggs.

olives

Trace and print **O** and **o**.

Ollie the octopus enjoys eating oranges.

Color each octopus leg a different color and his head orange.

P p

peach

Trace and print **P** and **p**.

P P P

p p

Three penguins and a puffin perform a play.
Find and circle the puffin.

Draw lines to match the letter pairs.

I   J   K   L

k   i   l   j

M   N   O   P

p   o   m   n

Qq

quince

Trace and print **Q** and **q**.

Q   Q

q   q

The queen bee quickly asks a question.
Follow the path to help the queen find her worker bees.

Rr

radishes

Trace and print **R** and **r**.

R R R

r r r

Rascally raccoons romp on a red rug.
Color all the **R** spaces **black**. Color all the **r** spaces **brown**.

S s

spaghetti

Trace and print **S** and **s**.

S   S   S

s   s

A soaked skunk swims in a stream.
Connect the dots and color in the stripe.

T t

tomato

Trace and print **T** and **t**.

T   T

t   t

Tim the tiger talks to the turtle.
Color the turtle teal.

I think we should take the trail.

Terrific!

ugli fruit

Trace and print **U** and **u**.

U U

u u

A beautiful unicorn rests under an umbrella.
Connect the dots.

V v

vegetables

Trace and print **V** and **v**.

A very relaxed vulture is on vacation.
Color the vulture violet.

watermelon

Trace and print **W** and **w**.

A warm whale swims in winter waters.
Draw a waterspout for the whale.

wax bean

Xx

Trace and print **X** and **x**.

Ray the x-ray fish meets Dexter.
Draw another x-ray fish.

Y y

yam

Trace and print **Y** and **y**.

Yes, there's a yak in our yard.
Color the yak yellow.

Zz

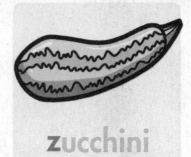

zucchini

Trace and print **Z** and **z**.

Z Z

z z

A zany zebra is at the zoo.
Draw **black** stripes on the zebra.

Draw lines to match the letter pairs.

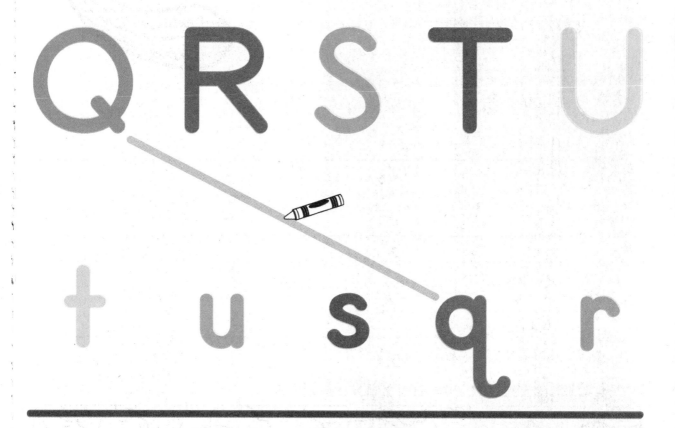

Q R S T U

t u s q r

V W X Y Z

x v z w y

Answers page 1

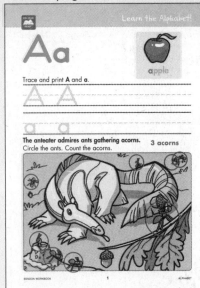

Answers page 2

Answers page 3

Answers page 4

Answers page 5

Answers page 6

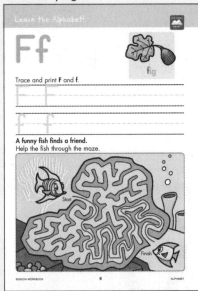

Answers page 8

Answers page 9

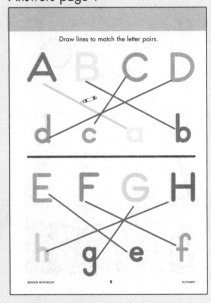

Answers page 10

Answers page 13

Ll — lemon

Trace and print L and l.

Liam the lion looks for Lucy the lioness.
Help the lion through the maze.

Answers page 15

Nn — noodles

Trace and print N and n.

5 eggs

Nancy the nightingale nears her nest.
Color and count the eggs.

Answers page 17

Pp — peach

Trace and print P and p.

Three penguins and a puffin perform a play.
Find and circle the puffin.

Answers page 18

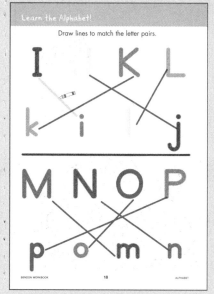

Draw lines to match the letter pairs.

I K L
k i j

M N O P
p o m n

Answers page 19

Qq — quince

Trace and print Q and q.

The queen bee quickly asks a question.
Follow the path to help the queen find her worker bees.

Answers page 20

Rr — radishes

Trace and print R and r.

Rascally raccoons romp on a red rug.
Color all the R spaces **black**. Color all the r spaces brown.

Answers page 21

Ss — spaghetti

Trace and print S and s.

A soaked skunk swims in a stream.
Connect the dots and color in the stripe.

Answers page 23

Uu — ugli fruit

Trace and print U and u.

A beautiful unicorn rests under an umbrella.
Connect the dots.

Answers page 29

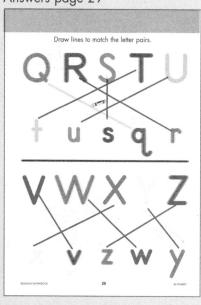

Draw lines to match the letter pairs.

Q R S T U
t u s q r

V W X Z
v z w y

Fun Family Activities

The following activities will provide additional review of the concepts explored on the workbook pages.

1. Puzzle Cards
Use 26 3" x 5" index cards. Write an uppercase alphabet letter on the left side of each card. Write the corresponding lowercase letter on the right side of the card. Cut the two letters apart using a different design for each card. Mix up the puzzle pieces. Help the child match the uppercase and lowercase letter pieces. The child may want to use the puzzle cuts as a guide until the upper and lowercase letters are memorized.

2. Memory Game
Select five to seven pairs of alphabet puzzle cards. Turn the cards upside down on the table. Ask the child to turn over two cards. If they are a matching letter set, the child keeps the cards and draws again until a match is not made. The unmatched cards are turned back over. The turn then proceeds to the player to the left. Play continues until all pairs are matched. The player with the most cards wins. Additional letter sets can be added for more challenge.

3. Visit the Library
Take the child to visit the local library. Find the alphabet book section. Help the child select different alphabet books to read. Ask your librarian if a young child can check out books with his or her own library card. If so, sign the child up for a card and let him or her select the books to take home for additional alphabet review.

4. Alphabet Guessing Game
Write a letter on a piece of paper and fold the paper in half so that the letter is hidden. Tell the child you are thinking of a letter that is between two letters. Let the child try to guess your letter. If the child's guess is incorrect, offer clues such as "It is a vowel" or "It makes the first sound in the word ____." When the child correctly guesses your letter, take a turn guessing his or her letter.

5. Reward Stickers
Use reward stickers to celebrate a job well done. You or the child can choose when to place a sticker on a specific page. Use a sticker as a reward when the child completes a page that requires extra care or is a little more difficult. The child can choose to place stickers on pages he or she is proud of completing.